MW00572939

THE

NEW-ENGLAND

PRIMER

IMPROVED

For the more eafy attaining the true
reading of Englifh.

TO WHICH IS ADDED

The Affembly of Divines, and
Mr. COTTON's *Catechifm*.

BOSTON:

Printed by EDWARD DRAPER, *at*
his Printing-Office, in *Newbury-*
Street, and *Sold* by JOHN BOYLE
in *Marlborough-Street.* 1777.

The New-England Primer

by John Cotton

This is a facsimile of the 1777 edition, which along with the primer included a catechism.

Note that as a facsimile, the edition will necessarily contain all of the defects of the original—but of course, also all of its charm.

Published by Suzeteo Enterprises, 2018.

All Rights Reserved

ISBN: 978-1-947844-34-6

Quantity discounts are available at bulk@suzeteo.com

The earliest information the publisher is *yet* able to collect, of the origin of the New England Primer, is contained in the following extract, from an Almanac now in the Library of the Massachusetts Historical Society, Boston.

IRA WEBSTER.

Boston, August 9th, 1844.

" *AN*

A L M A N A C K

Containing an Account of the *Cœleſtial Motions*, Aſpects, &c. For the year of the Chriſtian Empire, 1691.

By *Henry Newman*, Philomath.

Printed by *R. Pierce* for *Benjamin Harris* at the *London Coffee-Houſe in Boston*, 1691.

ADVERTISEMENT.

There is now in the Prefs, and will ſuddenly be extant, a Second Impreſſion of *the New England Primer enlarged*, to which is added, more *Directions for Spelling* : the *Prayer of K. Edward* the *6th.* and *Verſes made by Mr.* Rogers *the Martyr, left as a Legacy to his Children.*

Sold by *Benjamin Harris*, at the *London Coffee-House* in *Boſton*."

INTRODUCTION
TO THE PRESENT EDITION.

THE pious Baxter, who knew well the greater part of the Westminster Assembly of Divines, says, that the Christian world, since the days of the Apostles, never had a Synod of more excellent divines. The Assembly was convened in 1643; and was composed of *one hundred and twenty-one* divines, or presbyters, *thirty* lay assessors, and *five* commissioners from Scotland. It sat more than *five years and a half.*

Our Puritan Fathers brought the Shorter Catechism with them, across the ocean, and laid it on the same shelf with the family Bible. They taught it diligently to their children, every Sabbath. And while a few of their descendants, now in the *evening* of life, *remember* every question and answer; many, not yet advanced to life's *meridian*, can never *forget* when every Saturday *forenoon*, they had to take a regular catechising, in the common school, commencing with the a, b, c, *oaken-bench class*, "What is the chief end of man?"

If in this Catechism, the true and fundamental doctrines of the Gospel are expressed in fewer and better words, and definitions, than in any other summary, why ought we not *now* to *train up a child in the way he should go?*—why not *now*, put him in possession of the richest treasure that ever human wisdom and industry accumulated, to draw from?

HARTFORD, CONN.
PUBLISHED AND SOLD BY IRA WEBSTER. 1843
Stereotyped by R. H. HOBBS.

ADVERTISEMENT.

A Society of ladies was formed in Boston, in the time of Mr. Whitefield, for improvement in personal piety, and to pray for the extension of the Redeemer's Kingdom. The Society met weekly for prayer, "reading some sound and serious book," singing, and other exercises adapted to " spiritual edification." "We also agree," say they, "once a quarter, to spend the day in prayer and other duties of religion, our special errand at the throne of grace to ask for the outpouring of the Spirit of God on us, our families, and the world of mankind."—"Once a quarter, the exercises shall be so shortened, as to have room to ask ourselves the Assembly's Shorter Catechism, that so we may keep in our minds that excellent form of sound words." This edition of the New England Primer, is a reprint and fac-simile of one of those owned and used by that Society.

A community of Boston ladies of " the olden time," enrolling the bright names and embodying the choice influences of the mothers of this Israel—the Masons and the Waterses of hallowed memory—assembled quarterly to refresh their minds from this Primer. The fact needs no comment.*

N. B. This statement is from a lady who was a member of the above Society, and from the documents of the Society in her possession.

---

* " *Most valuable of every thing, is the education and principles drawn from the mother's knee.*"—UPSHUR.

CERTIFICATES.

At the request of the publisher, the following certificate has been furnished by a gentleman who has given much attention to the subject of early School Books and Catechisms, in this country.

" The edition of the New England Primer, published in 1843 by Mr. Ira Webster, of Hartford, is a correct reprint of the oldest copy of that remarkable work, of which I have any knowledge; perhaps the oldest copy now extant. All other reprints which I have seen, have been considerably altered—*modernized*—from the original.

    Cambridge, Oct. 20, 1849.   GEORGE LIVERMORE.''

    Communicated by the Rev. Thomas Williams:

" The edition of the New England Primer, which has been published by Mr. Ira Webster, of Hartford, in the year 1843, is the only genuine and correct edition of that valuable and wonderful book that has been to be obtained for many years. It is probably more than fifty years since there has been printed a complete and correct edition of the Primer, except the one printed by Mr. Webster. His edition is an exact copy of the Primer that was used by families and schools in my youth, sixty years ago, and I suppose it had been used for fifty or a hundred years before that time. The genuine copy of the Primer, on account of its antiquity, and its extensive usefulness in former years, has now become an object of interesting and beneficial curiosity.''   THOMAS WILLIAMS.

    Plymouth, Massachusetts, June 23, *A. D.* 1844.

    We, the subscribers, concur in the preceding statements.

                      THOMAS ROBBINS,
                      JOEL HAWES,
Hartford, Oct. 30, 1849.   T. H. GALLAUDET.

The publisher of this edition, from one of 1777—(wishing to obtain information of still older copies,) would say that he has in his possession three Primers, two printed in Boston, 1770, 1777, and one in Providence, 1775, *all the same*, after the title page.

The Honorable JOHN HANCOCK, Efq;
Prefident of the *American* CONGRESS.

A Divine Song of Praife to G O D, for a Child,
by the Rev. Dr. W A T T S.

*H*OW *glorious is our heavenly King,*
Who reigns above the Sky!
How fhall a Child prefume to fing
His dreadful Majefty!

How great his Power is none can tell,
Nor think how large his Grace:
Nor men below, nor Saints that dwell
On high before his Face.

Nor Angels that ftand round the Lord,
Can fearch his fecret will;
But they perform his heav'nly Word,
And fing his Praifes ftill.

Then let me join this holy Train,
And my firft Off'rings bring;
The eternal GOD will not difdain
To hear an Infant fing.

My Heart refolves, my Tongue obeys,
And Angels fhall rejoice,
To hear their mighty Maker's Praife,
Sound from a feeble Voice.

THE

NEW-ENGLAND

PRIMER

IMPROVED

For the more eafy attaining the true
reading of Englifh.

TO WHICH IS ADDED

The Affembly of Divines, and
Mr. COTTON's *Catechifm.*

BOSTON:

Printed by EDWARD DRAPER, *at*
his Printing-Office, in *Newbury-*
Street, and *Sold* by JOHN BOYLE
in *Marlborough-Street.* 1777.

The young INFANT's or CHILD's morning Prayer. *From* Dr. WATTS.

ALMIGHTY God the Maker of every Thing in Heaven and Earth; the Darkness goes away, and the Day light comes at thy Command. Thou art good and doeſt good continually.

I thank thee that thou haſt taken ſuch Care of me this Night, and that I am alive and well this Morning.

Save me, O God, from Evil, all this Day long, and let me love and ſerve thee forever, for the Sake of Jeſus Chriſt thy Son. AMEN.

The INFANT's or young CHILD's Evening Prayer. *From* Dr. WATTS.

O LORD God who knoweſt all Things, thou ſeeſt me by Night as well as by Day.

I pray thee for Chriſt's Sake, forgive me whatſoever I have done amiſs this Day, and keep me all this Night, while I am aſleep.

I deſire to lie down under thy Care, and to abide forever under thy Bleſſing, for thou art a God of all Power and everlaſting Mercy. AMEN.

a b c d e f g h i j k l m

n o p q r ſ s t u v

w x y z &.

Vowels.

a e i o u y.

Conſonants.

b c d f g h j k l m n p q r ſ s t v w x z

Double Letters.

ct ff fi fl ffi ffl ſh ſi ſſi fl ff ſt

Italick Letters.

Aa Bb Cc Dd Ee Ff Gg Hh
Ii Jj Kk Ll Mm Nn Oo Pp Qq
Rr Sſs Tt Uu Vv Ww Xx Yy Zz

Italick Double Letters.

ct ff fi ffi fl ffl ſh ſi ſſ ſſi ſl ſt.

1*

Great Letters.

A B C D E F G H I J K L M N O

P Q R S T U W X Y Z.

Ab	eb	ib	ob	ub
ac	ec	ic	oc	uc
ad	ed	id	od	ud
af	ef	if	of	uf
ag	eg	ig	og	ug
aj	ej	ij	oj	uj
ak	ek	ik	ok	uk
al	el	il	ol	ul
am	em	im	om	um
an	en	in	on	un
ap	ep	ip	op	up
ar	er	ir	or	ur
as	es	is	os	us
at	et	it	ot	ut
av	ev	iv	ov	uv
ax	ex	ix	ox	ux
az	ez	iz	oz	uz

Eaſy

Eaſy Syllables, &c.

Ba	be	bi	bo	bu
ca	ce	ci	co	cu
da	de	di	do	du
fa	fe	fi	fo	fu
ga	ge	gi	go	gu
ha	he	hi	ho	hu
ja	je	ji	jo	ju
ka	ke	ki	ko	ku
la	le	li	lo	lu
ma	me	mi	mo	mu
na	ne	ni	no	nu
pa	pe	pi	po	pu
ra	re	ri	ro	ru
ſa	ſe	ſi	ſo	ſu
ta	te	ti	to	tu
va	ve	vi	vo	vu
wa	we	wi	wo	wu
ya	ye	yi	yo	yu
za	ze	zi	zo	zu

Words of one Syllable.

Age	all	ape	are
Babe	beef	beſt	bold
Cat	cake	crown	cup
Deaf	dead	dry	dull

Words of one Syllable.

Eat	ear	eggs	eyes
Face	feet	filh	foul
Gate	good	grafs	great
Hand	hat	head	heart
Ice	ink	ifle	jobb
Kick	kind	kneel	know
Lamb	lame	land	long
Made	mole	moon	mouth
Name	night	noife	noon
Oak	once	one	ounce
Pain	pair	pence	pound
Quart	queen	quick	quilt
Rain	raife	rofe	run
Saint	fage	falt	faid
Take	talk	time	throat
Vain	vice	vile	view
Way	wait	wafte	would

Words of two Syllables.

Ab-fent	ab-hor	a-pron	au-thor
Ba-bel	be-came	be-guile	bold-ly
Ca-pon	cel-lar	con-ftant	cub-board
Dai-ly	de-pend	di-vers	du-ty
Ea-gle	ea-ger	en-close	e-ven
Fa-ther	fa-mous	fe-male	fu-ture
Ga-ther	gar-den	gra-vy	glo-ry

Words of two Syllables.

Hei-nous	hate-ful	hu-mane	hus-band
In-fant	in-deed	in-cence	i-fland
Ja-cob	jeal-ous	juf-tice	ju-lep
La-bour	la-den	la-dy	la-zy
Ma-ny	ma-ry	mo-tive	mu-fick

Words of three Syllables.

A-bu-fing	a-mend-ing	ar-gu-ment
Bar-ba-rous	be-ne-fit	beg-gar-ly
Cal-cu-late	can-dle-stick	con-foun-ded
Dam-ni-fy	dif-fi-cult	drow-fi-nefs
Ea-ger-ly	em-ploy-ing	evi-dence
Fa-cul-ty	fa-mi-ly	fu-ne-ral
Gar-de-ner	glo-ri-ous	gra-ti-tude
Hap-pi-ness	har-mo-ny	ho-li-nefs

Words of four Syllables.

A-bi-li-ty	ac-com-pa-ny	af-fec-ti-on
Be-ne-fi-ted	be-a-ti-tude	be-ne-vo-lent
Ca-la-mi-ty	ca-pa-ci-ty	ce-re-mo-ny
De-li-ca-cy	di-li-gent-ly	du-ti-ful-ly
E-dy-fy-ing	e-ver-laft-ing	e-vi-dent-ly
Fe-bru-a-ry	fi-de-li-ty	for-mi-da-bly
Ge-ne-ral-ly	glo-ri-fy-ing	gra-ci-ous-ly

Words of five Syllables.

A-bo-mi-na-ble	ad-mi-ra-ti-on
Be-ne-dic-ti-on	be-ne-fi-ci-al
Ce-le-bra-ti-on	con-fo-la-ti-on
De-cla-ra-ti-on	de-di-ca-ti-on
E-du-ca-ti-on	ex-hor-ta-ti-on
For-ni-ca-ti-on	fer-men-ta-ti-on
Ge-ne-ra-ti-on	ge-ne-ro-fi-ty

Words of fix Syllables.

A-bo-mi-na-ti-on	Gra-ti-fi-ca-ti-on
Be-ne-fi-ci-al-ly	Hu-mi-li-a-ti-on
Con-ti-nu-a-ti-on	I-ma-gi-na-ti-on
De-ter-mi-na-ti-on	Mor-ti-fi-ca-ti-on
E-di-fi-ca-ti-on	Pu-ri-fi-ca-ti-on
Fa-mi-li-a-ri-ty	Qua-li-fi-ca-ti-on

A Leſſon for Children.

Pray to God.	Call no ill names.
Love God.	Uſe no ill words.
Fear God.	Tell no lies.
Serve God.	Hate Lies.
Take not God's	Speak the Truth.
Name in vain.	Spend your Time well
Do not Swear.	Love your School.
Do not Steal.	Mind your Book.
Cheat not in your play.	Strive to learn.
Play not with bad boys.	Be not a Dunce.

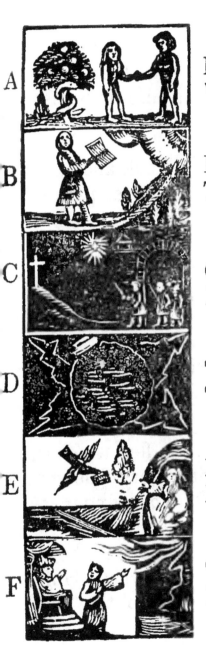

A   In A D A M's Fall
We finned all.

B   Heaven to find,
The Bible Mind.

C   Chrift crucify'd
For finners dy'd.

D   The Deluge drown'd
The Earth around.

E   E L I J A H hid
By Ravens fed.

F   The judgment made
F E L I X afraid.

G   As runs the Glass,
Our Life doth pass.

H   My Book and Heart
Must never part.

I   JOB feels the Rod,—
Yet bleſſes GOD.

K   Proud Korah's troop
Was ſwallowed up

L   LOT fled to *Zoar*,
Saw fiery Shower
On *Sodom* pour.

M   MOSES was he
Who *Israel's* Hoſt
Led thro' the Sea.

N | Noah did view
The old world & new

O | Young Obadias,
David, Josias
All were pious.

P | Peter deny'd
His Lord and cry'd.

Q | Queen Esther sues
And saves the *Jews*.

R | Young pious Ruth,
Left all for Truth.

S | Young Sam'l dear
The Lord did fear.

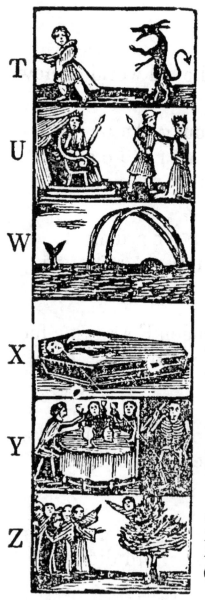

T — Young TIMOTHY
Learnt fin to fly.

U — VASTHI for Pride,
Was fet afide.

W — Whales in the Sea,
GOD's Voice obey.

X — XERXES did die,
And fo muft I.

Y — While youth do chear
Death may be near.

Z — ZACCHEUS he
Did climb the Tree
Our Lord to fee.

WHO was the firſt man ?   *Adam.*
    Who was the firſt woman ?   *Eve.*
Who was the firſt Murderer ?   *Cain.*
Who was the firſt Martyr ?   *Abel.*
Who was the firſt Tranſlated ?   *Enoch.*
Who was the oldeſt Man ?   *Methuſelah.*
Who built the Ark ?   *Noah.*
Who was the Patienteſt Man ?   *Job.*
Who was the Meekeſt Man ?   *Moſes.*
Who led *Iſrael* into *Canaan* ?   *Joſhua.*
Who was the ſtrongest Man ?   *Sampſon.*
Who killed *Goliah* ?   *David.*
Who was the wiſeſt Man ?   *Solomon.*
Who was in the Whale's Belly ?   *Jonah.*
Who ſaves loſt Men ?   *Jeſus Chriſt.*
Who is *Jeſus Chriſt* ?   *The Son of God.*
Who was the Mother of *Chriſt* ?   *Mary.*
Who betrayed his Maſter ?   *Judas.*
Who denied his Maſter ?   *Peter.*
Who was the firſt Chriſtian Martyr ? *Stephen.*
Who was chief Apoſtle of the *Gentiles* ? *Paul.*

The Infant's Grace before and after Meat.

BLESS me, O Lord, and let my food ſtrengthen me to ſerve thee, for Jesus Chriſt's ſake.   AMEN.

I Deſire to thank God who gives me food to eat every day of my life.   AMEN.

WHAT's right and good now fhew me Lord, and lead me by thy grace and word. Thus fhall I be a child of God, and love and fear thy hand and rod.

An Alphabet of Leffons for Youth.

A Wife fon maketh a glad father, but a foolifh fon is the heavinefs of his mother.

B Etter is a little with the fear of the Lord, than great treasure & trouble therewith.

C Ome unto Chrift all ye that labor and are heavy laden and he will give you reft.

D O not the abominable thing which I hate faith the Lord.

E Xcept a man be born again, he cannot fee the kingdom of God.

F Oolifhnefs is bound up in the heart of a child, but the rod of correction fhall drive it far from him.

G ODLINESS is profitable unto all things, having the promife of the life that now is, and that which is to come.

H OLINESS becomes G O D's houfe for ever.

I T is good for me to draw near unto GOD.

KEEP thy heart with all diligence, for out of it are the issues of life.

LIARS shall have their part in the lake which burns with fire and brimstone.

MANY are the afflictions of the rightous, but the L O R D delivereth them out of them all.

NOW is the accepted time, now is the day of salvation.

OUT of the abundance of the heart the mouth speaketh.

PRAY to thy Father which is in secret; and thy Father which sees in secret shall reward thee openly.

QUIT you like men, be strong, stand fast in the faith.

REMEMBER thy Creator in the days of thy youth.

SEest thou a man wise in his own conceit, there is more hope of a fool than of him.

TRUST in God at all times, ye people, pour out your hearts before him.

UPON the wicked, God shall rain an horrible tempest.

WO to the wicked, it shall be ill with him, for the reward of his hands shall be given him.

E**X**HORT one another daily while it is called to day, left any of you be hardened thro' the deceitfulnefs of fin.

YOUNG men ye have overcome the wicked one.

Z Eal hath confumed me, becaufe thy enemies have forgotten the word of God.

The LORD's Prayer.

OUR Father which art in heaven, hallowed be thy name. Thy kingdom come. Thy will be done on earth as it is heaven. Give us this day our daily bread. And forgive us our debts as we forgive our debtors. And lead us not into temptation. But deliver us from evil. For thine is the kingdom, the power and the glory, forever. AMEN.

The C R E E D.

I BELIEVE in God the Father Almighty Maker of heaven and earth, and in Jefus Chrift his only Son our Lord, which was conceived by the Holy Ghoft, born of the Virgin Mary, fuffered under Pontius Pilate, was crucified, dead and buried. He defcended into hell. The third day he arofe again from the dead, and afcended into heaven, and fitteth on the right hand of God, the Father,

Almighty. From thence he ſhall come to judge both the quick and the dead. I believe in the Holy Ghoſt, the Holy Catholic Church, the communion of Saints, the forgivenefs of fins, the refurrection of the body, and the life everlaſting. AMEN.

Dr. WATTS's *Cradle Hymn.*

HUSH my dear, lie ſtill and ſlumber,
    holy angels guard thy bed,
Heavenly bleſſings without number,
    gently falling on thy head.
Sleep my babe, thy food and raiment
    houſe and home thy friends provide,
All without thy care or payment,
    all thy wants are well ſupply'd.
How much better thou'rt attended,
    than the Son of God could be,
When from heaven he deſcended,
    and became a child like thee.
Soft and eaſy is thy cradle,
    coarſe and hard thy Saviour lay,
When his birth-place was a ſtable,
    and his ſofteſt bed was hay.
Bleſſed Babe! what glorious features,
    ſpotlefs fair, divinely bright!!
Muſt he dwell with brutal creatures,

how could angels bear the fight!
Was there nothing but a manger,
  curfed finners could afford,
To receive the heavenly ftranger;
  did they thus affront their Lord.
Soft my child I did not chide thee,
  tho' my fong may found too hard;
'Tis thy mother fits befide thee,
  and her arms fhall be thy guard.
Yet to read the fhameful ftory,
  how the Jews abus'd their King,
How they ferv'd the Lord of glory,
  makes me angry while I fing.
See the kinder fhepherds round him,
  telling wonders from the fky;
There they fought him, there they found him,
  with his Virgin Mother by.
See the lovely Babe a dreffing;
  lovely Infant how he fmil'd!
When he wept, the Mother's bleffing
  sooth'd and hufh'd the holy child.
Lo! he flumbers in his manger,
  where the horned oxen fed;
Peace my darling here's no danger,
  here's no Ox a near thy bed.
'Twas to fave thee, child from dying
  fave my dear from burning flame,

Bitter groans and endlefs crying,
   that thy bleft Redeemer came.
May'ft thou live to know and fear him,
   truft and love him all thy days!
Then go dwell for ever near him,
   fee his face and fing his praife.
I could give thee thoufand kiffes,
   hoping what I moft defire:
Not a mother's fondeft wifhes,
   can to greater joys afpire.

VERSES *for Children.*

THOUGH I am young a little one,
   If I can fpeak and go alone,
Then I muft learn to know the Lord,
And learn to read his holy word.
'Tis time to feek to God and pray
For what I want for every day:
I have a precious foul to fave,
And I a mortal body have,
Tho' I am young yet I may die,
And haften to eternity:
There is a dreadful fiery hell,
Where wicked ones must always dwell:
There is a heaven full of joy,
Where godly ones must always ftay:
To one of thefe my foul must fly,
 As in a moment when I die:

2

When God that made me, calls me home,
I muſt not stay I muſt be gone.
He gave me life, and gives me breath,
And he can ſave my ſoul from death,
By JESUS CHRIST my only Lord,
According to his holy word.
He clothes my back and makes me warm:
He ſaves my fleſh and bones from harm.
He gives me bread and milk and meat
And all I have that's good to eat.
When I am ſick, he if he pleaſe,
Can make me well and give me eaſe:
He gives me ſleep and quiet reſt,
Whereby my body is refreſh'd
The Lord is good and kind to me,
And very thankful I muſt be:
I muſt obey and love and fear him,
By faith in Chriſt I muſt draw near him.
I muſt not ſin as others do,
Leſt I lie down in ſorrow too:
For God is angry every day,
With wicked ones who go aſtray,
All ſinful words I must reſtrain:
I muſt not take God's name in vain.
I muſt not work, I muſt not play,
Upon God's holy ſabbath day.
And if my parents ſpeak the word,

I muſt obey them in the Lord.
Nor ſteal, nor lie, nor ſpend my days,
In idle tales and fooliſh plays,
I muſt obey my Lord's commands,
Do ſomething with my little hands :
Remember my creator now,
In youth while time will it allow.
Young SAMUEL that little child,
He ſerv'd the Lord, liv'd undefil'd;
Him in his ſervice God employ'd,
While ELI's wicked children dy'd :
When wicked children mocking ſaid,
To a good man, *Go up bald head*,
God was diſpleas'd with them and ſent
Two bears which them in pieces rent,
I muſt not like theſe children vile,
Diſpleaſe my God, myſelf defile.
Like young ABIJAH, I muſt ſee,
That good things may be found in me,
Young King JOSIAH, that bleſſed youth,
He ſought the Lord and lov'd the truth ;
He like a King did act his part,
And follow'd God with all his heart.
The little children they did ſing,
Hoſannahs to their heavenly King.
That bleſſed child young TIMOTHY,
Did learn God's word moſt heedfully.

It feem'd to be his recreation,
Which made him wife unto falvation :
By faith in Chrift which he had gain'd
With prayers and tears that faith unfeign'd.
Thefe good examples were for me ;
Like thefe good children I must be.
Give me true faith in Chrift my Lord,
Obedience to his holy word,
No word is in the world like thine,
There's none fo pure, fweet and divine.
From thence let me thy will behold,
And love thy word above fine gold.
Make my heart in thy ftatutes found,
And make my faith and love abound.
Lord circumcife my heart to love thee :
And nothing in this world above thee :
Let me behold thy pleafed face,
And make my foul to grow in grace,
And in the knowledge of my Lord
And Saviour Chrift, and of his word.

Another.

AWAKE, arife, behold thou haft,
Thy life a leaf, thy breath a blaft,
At night lay down prepar'd to have
Thy fleep, thy death, thy bed, thy grave.
LORD if thou lengthen out my days,
Then let my heart fo fixed be,

That I may lengthen out thy praise,
And never turn aside from thee.
 So in my end I shall rejoice,
In thy salvation joyful be;
My soul shall say with loud glad voice,
JEHOVAH who is like to thee?
 Who takest the lambs into thy arms,
And gently leadest those with young,
Who savest children from all harms,
Lord, I will praise thee with my song.
 And when my days on earth shall end,
And I go hence and be here no more,
Give me eternity to spend,
My G O D to praise forever more.

Another.

Good children must,

Fear God all day,	Love Christ alway,
Parents obey,	In secret pray,
No false thing say,	Mind little play,
By no sin stray,	Make no delay,

In doing good.

Another.

I In the burying place may see
 Graves shorter there than I,
From death's arrest no age is free
 Young children too must die.
My God may such an awful sight,

Awakening be to me!
Oh! that by early grace I might
  For death prepared be.

Another.

NOW I lay me down to take my sleep,
  I pray the Lord my soul to keep,
If I should die before I wake,
I pray the Lord my soul to take.

Another.

FIrst in the morning when thou dost awake,
  To God for his grace thy petition make,
Some heavenly petition use daily to say,
That the God of heaven may bless thee alway.

Duty to God and our neighbour.

LOVE God with all your soul & strength,
  With all your heart and mind;
And love your neighbour as yourself,
  Be faithful, just and kind.
Deal with another as you'd have
  Another deal with you:
What you're unwilling to receive,
  Be sure you never do.

Our Saviour's Golden Rule.

BE you to others kind and true,
  As you'd have others be to you:
And neither do nor say to men,
  Whate'er you would not take again.

The Sum of the ten Commandments.

WITH all thy foul love God above,
    And as thyfelf thy neighbour love.
   Advice to Youth. Eccle. xii.

NOW in the heat of youthful blood,
    Remember your Creator God;
Behold the months come haft'ning on,
When you fhall fay, *My joys are gone.*

  Behold the aged finner goes
Laden with guilt and heavy woes,
Down to the regions of the dead,
With endlefs curfes on his head.

  The duft returns to duft again,
The foul in agonies of pain,
Afcends to God not there to dwell,
But hears her doom and finks to hell.
Eternal King I fear thy name,
Teach me to know how frail I am,
And when my foul muft hence remove,
Give me a manfion in thy love.

Remember thy Creator in the days of thy youth.

CHILDREN your great Creator fear,
    To him your homage pay,
While vain employments fire your blood,
    And lead your thoughts aftray.
The due remembrance of his name
    Your first regard requires :

Till your breaſt glows with ſacred **love,**
    Indulge no meaner fires.
Secure his favour, and be wiſe,
    Before theſe cheerleſs days,
When age comes on, when mirth's **no more**
    And health and ſtrength decays.

Some proper Names of M E N *and* W O M E N,
    to teach Children to ſpell their own.

Men's Names.

A Dam, Abel, Abraham,
Amos, Aaron,
Abijah, Andrew,
Alexander, Anthony,
Bartholomew,
Benjamin, Barnabas,
Benoni, Barzillai,
Caleb, Cæſar,
Charles, Christopher,
Clement, Cornelius,
David, Daniel,
Ephraim, Edward,
Edmund, Ebenezer,
Elijah, Eliphalet,
Eliſha, Eleazer,
Elihu, Ezekiel,
Elias, Elizur,
Frederick, Francis,
Gilbert, Giles,
George, Gamalial,
Gideon, Gerſhom,
Heman, Henry,
Hezekiah, Hugh,
John, Jonas, Iſaac,
Jacob, Jared, Job,
James, Jonathan,
Iſrael, Joſeph,
Jeremiah, Joſhua,
Joſiah, Jedediah,
Jabez, Joel, Judah,
Lazarus, Luke,
Mathew, Michael,
Moſes, Malachi,
Nathaniel, Nathan,

Nicholas, Noadiah, Nehemiah, Noah, Obadiah, Ozias, Paul, Peter, Philip, Phineas, Peletiah, Ralph, Richard, Samuel, Sampſon, Stephen, Solomon, Seth, Simeon, Saul,

Shem, Shubal, Timothy, Thomas, Titus, Theophilus, Uriah, Uzzah, Walter, William, Xerxes, Xenophon, Zachariah, Zebdiel, Zedekiah, Zadock, Zebulon, Zebediah,

Women's Names.

Abigail, Anne, Alice, Anna, Bethiah, Bridget, Cloe, Charity, Deborah, Dorothy, Dorcas, Dinah, Damaris, Elizabeth, Eſther, Eunice, Eleanor, Frances, Flora, Grace, Gillet, Hannah, Huldah, Hepzibah, Henrietta, Hagar. Joanna, Jane, Jamima, Iſabel,

Judith, Jennet, Katharine, Katura, Kezia, Lydia, Lucretia, Lucy, Louis, Lettice, Mary, Margaret, Martha, Mehitable, Marcy, Merial, Patience, Phylis, Phebe, Priſcilla, Rachel, Rebecca, Ruth, Rhode, Roſe, Sarah, Suſanna, Tabitha, Tameſin, Urſula, Zipporah, Zibiah.

2*

M R. JOHN ROGERS, minister of the gospel in *London*, was the first martyr in Queen MARY's reign, and was burnt at *Smithfield, February* 14, 1554.—His wife with nine small children, and one at her breast following him to the stake; with which sorrowful sight he was not in the least daunted, but with wonderful patience died courageously for the gospel of JESUS CHRIST.

Some few days before his death, he wrote the following Advice to his Children.

GIVE ear my children to my words
   Whom God hath dearly bought,
Lay up his laws within your heart,
   and print them in your thoughts.
I leave you here a little book
   for you to look upon,
That you may fee your father's face
   when he is dead and gone :
Who for the hope of heavenly things
   While he did here remain,
Gave over all his golden years
   to prifon and to pain.
Where I, among my iron bands,
   inclofed in the dark,
Not many days before my death,
   I did compofe this work :
And for example to your youth,
   to whom I wifh all good,
I fend you here God's perfect truth,
   and feal it with my blood.
To you my heirs of earthly things :
   which I do leave behind,
That you may read and underftand
   and keep it in your mind.
That as you have been heirs of that

that once fhall wear away,
You alfo may poffefs that part,
   which never fhall decay.
Keep always God before your eyes,
   with all your whole intent,
Commit no fin in any wife,
   keep his commandment.
Abhor that arrant whore of R o m e,
   and all her blafphemies,
And drink not of her curfed cup,
   obey not her decrees.
Give honor to your mother dear,
   remember well her pain,
And recompence her in her age,
   with the like love again.
Be always ready for her help,
   and let her not decay,
Remember well your father all,
   who would have been your ftay.
Give of your portion to the poor,
   as riches do arife,
And from the needy naked foul,
   turn not away your eyes:
For he that doth not hear the cry
   of thofe that ftand in need,
Shall cry himfelf and not be heard,
   when he does hope to fpeed.

If GOD hath given you increafe,
    and bleffed well your ftore,
Remember you are put in truft,
    and fhould relieve the poor.
Beware of foul and filthy luft,
    let fuch things have no place,
Keep clean your veffels in the LORD,
    that he may you embrace.
Ye are the temples of the LORD,
    for you are dearly bought,
And they that do defile the fame,
    fhall furely come to nought.
Be never proud by any means,
    build not your houfe too high,
But always have before your eyes,
    that you are born to die.
Defraud not him that hired is,
    your labour to fuftain,
But pay him ftill without delay,
    his wages for his pain.
And as you would that other men
    againft you fhould proceed,
Do you the fame to them again,
    when they do ftand in need.
Impart your portion to the poor,
    in money and in meat

And fend the feeble fainting foul,
   of that which you do eat.
Afk counfel always of the wife,
   give ear unto the end,
And ne'er refufe the fweet rebuke
   of him that is thy friend.
Be always thankful to the LORD,
   with prayer and with praife,
Begging of him to blefs your work,
   and to direct your ways.
Seek firft, I fay, the living GOD,
   and always him adore,
And then be fure that he will blefs,
   your bafket and your ftore.
And I befeech Almighty GOD,
   replenifh you with grace,
That I may meet you in the heavens,
   and fee you face to face.
And though the fire my body burns,
   contrary to my kind,
That I cannot enjoy your love
   according to my mind :
Yet I do hope that when the heavens
   fhall vanifh like a fcroll,
I fhall fee you in perfect fhape,
   in body and in foul.
And that I may enjoy your love,

and you enjoy the land,
I do befeech the living LORD,
   to hold you in his hand.
Though here my body be adjudg'd
   in flaming fire to fry,
My foul I truft, will ftraight afcend
   to live with GOD on high.
What though this carcafe fmart awhile
   what though this life decay,
My foul I hope will be with GOD,
   and live with him for aye.
I know I am a finner born,
   from the original,
And that I do deferve to die
   by my fore-father's fall :
But by our S A V I O U R's precious blood,
   which on the crofs was fpilt,
Who freely offer'd up his life,
   to fave our fouls from guilt :
I hope redemption I fhall have,
   and all who in him truft,
When I fhall fee him face to face,
   and live among the juft.
Why then fhould I fear death's grim look
   fince CHRIST for me did die,
For King and *Cæfar*, rich and poor,
   the force of death muft try

When I am chained to the ſtake,
   and ſagots girt me round,
Then pray the LORD my ſoul in heaven
   may be with glory crown'd.
Come welcome death the end of fears,
   I am prepar'd to die :
Thoſe earthly flames will ſend my ſoul
   up to the Lord on high.
Farewell my children to the world,
   where you muſt yet remain ;
The LORD of hoſts be your defence,
   'till we do meet again.
Farewell my true and loving wife,
   my children and my friends,
I hope in heaven to ſee you all,
   when all things have their end.
If you go on to ſerve the LORD,
   as you have now begun,
You ſhall walk ſafely all your days,
   until your life be done.
GOD grant you ſo to end your days,
   as he ſhall think it beſt,
That I may meet you in the heavens,
   where I do hope to reſt.

OUR days begin with trouble here,
   our life is but a ſpan,

And cruel death is always near,
　　ſo frail a thing is man.
Then ſow the ſeeds of grace whilſt young,
　　that when thou com'ſt to die,
Thou may'ſt ſing forth that triumph ſong,
　　Death where's thy victory.

Choice Sentences.

1. P R A Y i N G will make us leave ſinning, or ſinning will make us leave praying.

2. O U R weakneſs and inabilities break not the bond of our duties.

3. W H A T we are aſraid to ſpeak before men, we ſhould be afraid to think before GOD.

Learn theſe four lines by heart.

H A V E communion with few,
　　Be intimate with ONE,
Deal juſtly with all,
Speak evil of none.

A G U R's Prayer.

R E M O V E far from me vanities and lies ; give me neither poverty nor riches ; feed me with food convenient for me : leſt I be full and deny thee, and ſay, Who is the Lord ? Or leſt I be poor and ſteal and take the name of my GOD in vain.

THE SHORTER
CATECHISM,

Agreed upon by the Reverend Aſſembly of
DIVINES at *Weſtminſter.*

Queſt. *W*°*HAT is the chief end of man?*
Anſ. Man's chief end is to
glorify God and enjoy him forever.

Q. 2. *What rule hath God given to direct us how we may glorify and enjoy him?*

A. The word of God which is contained
in the ſcriptures of the old and new teſtament is the only rule to direct us how we
may glorify God and enjoy him.

Q.3. *What do the ſcriptures principally teach?*

A. The ſcriptures principally teach what
man is to believe concerning God, and what
duty God requireth of man.

Q. 4. *What is God?*

A. God is a ſpirit, infinite, eternal, and
unchangeable, in his being, wiſdom, power,
holineſs, juſtice, goodneſs and truth.

Q. 5. *Are there more Gods than one?*

A. There is but ONE only, the living and true GOD.

Q. 6. *How many persons are there in the God-head?*

A. There are three perfons in the God-head, the Father, the Son, and the Holy Ghoft, and thefe three are one GOD, the fame in fubftance, equal in power and glory.

Q. 7. *What are the decrees of God?*

A. The decrees of God are his eternal purpofe, according to the counfel of his own will, whereby for his own glory he hath fore-ordained whatfoever comes to pafs.

Q. 8. *How doth God execute his decrees?*

A. God executeth his decrees in the works of creation and providence.

Q. 9. *What is the work of creation?*

A. The work of creation is God's making all things of nothing by the word of his power, in the fpace of fix days, and all very good.

Q. 10. *How did God create man?*

A. God created man male & female after his own image, in knowledge, righteoufnefs and holinefs, with dominion over the creatures

Q. 11. *What are God's works of providence?*

A. God's works of providence are his moft holy, wife and powerful, preferving & governing all his creatures and all their actions.

Q. 12. *What special act of providence did God exercise towards man in the estate wherein he was created?*

A. When God had created man, he entered into a covenant of life with him upon condition of perfect obedience, forbidding him to eat of the tree of knowledge of good and evil, upon pain of death.

Q. 13. *Did our first parents continue in the estate wherein they were created?*

A. Our first parents being left to the freedom of their own will, fell from the estate wherein they were created, by sinning against God.

Q. 14. *What is sin?*

A. Sin is any want of conformity unto, or transgression of the law of God.

Q. 15. *What was the sin whereby our first parents fell from the estate wherein they were created?*

A. The sin whereby our first parents fell from the estate wherein they were created, was their eating the forbidden fruit.

Q. 16, *Did all mankind fall in Adam's first transgression?*

A. The covenant being made with *Adam*, not only for himself, but for his posterity, all mankind defcending from him by ordinary generation, finned in him, and fell with him in his firft tranfgreffion.

Q. 17. *Into what eftate did the fall bring mankind ?*

A. The fall brought mankind into an estate of fin and mifery.

Q. 18. *Wherein confifts the finfulnefs of that eftate whereinto man fell ?*

A. The finfulnefs of that eftate whereinto man fell, confifts in the guilt of *Adam's* firft fin, the want of original righteousnefs, & the corruption of his whole nature, which is commonly called original fin, together with all actual tranfgreffions which proceed from it.

Q. 19. *What is the mifery of that eftate whereinto man fell ?*

A. All mankind by the fall loft communion with God, are under his wrath & curfe, and fo made liable to the miferies in this life, to death itfelf, & to the pains of hell forever.

Q. 20. *Did God leave all mankind to perifh in the ftate of fin and mifery ?*

A. God having out of his mere good pleafure from all eternity elected fome to everlafting life, did enter into a covenant of grace, to deliver them out of a ftate of fin and mifery, and to bring them into a ftate of falvation by a Redeemer.

Q. 21. *Who is the Redeemer of God's elect?*

A. The only Redeemer of God's elect, is the Lord Jefus Chrift, who being the eternal Son of God, became man, and fo was, and continues to be God and man, in two diftinct natures, and one perfon forever.

Q. 22. *How did Chrift being the Son of God become man ?*

A. Chrift the Son of God became man by taking to himfelf a true body and a refonable foul, being conceived by the power of the Holy Ghoft, in the womb of the virgin *Mary*, and born of her, and yet without fin.

Q. 23. *What offices doth Chrift execute as our Redeemer ?*

A. Chrift as our Redeemer executes the office of a prophet, of a prieft, & of a king, both in his eftate of humiliation and exaltation.

Q. 24. *How doth Chrift execute the office of a prophet ?*

A. Chrift executeth the office of a prophet in revealing to us by his word and fpirit, the will of God for our falvation.

Q. 25. *How doth Chrift execute the office of a prieft ?*

A. Chriſt executeth the office of a prieſt in his once offering up himſelf a ſacrifice to ſatisfy divine juſtice, and reconcile us to God, and in making continual interceſſion for us.

Q. 26. *How doth Chriſt execute the office of a king?*

A. Chriſt executeth the office of a king in ſubduing us to himſelf, in ruling and defending us, and in reſtraining and conquering all his and our enemies.

Q 27 *Wherein did Chriſt's humiliation conſiſt?*

A. Chriſt's humiliation conſiſted in his being born and that in a low condition, made under the law, undergoing the miſeries of this life, the wrath of God, and the curſed death of the crofs, in being buried and continuing under the power of death for a time.

Q. 28. *Wherein conſiſts Chriſt's exaltation?*

A. Chriſt's exaltation conſiſteth in his riſing again from the dead on the third day, in aſcending up into heaven, and ſitting at the right hand of God the Father, and in coming to judge the world at the last day.

Q. 29. *How are we made partakers of the redemption purchased by Chriſt?*

A. We are made partakers of the redemption purchaſed by Chriſt by the effectual application of it to us by his holy Spirit.

Q. 30. *How doth the Spirit apply to us the redemption purchaſed by Chriſt?*

A. The Spirit applieth to us the redemption purchaſed by Chriſt, by working faith in us, and thereby uniting us to Chriſt in our effectual calling.

Q. 31. *What is effectual calling?*

A. Effectual calling is the work of God's Spirit, whereby convincing us of our ſin and miſery, enlightening our minds in the knowledge of Chriſt, and renewing our wills, he doth perſuade and enable us to embrace Jeſus Chriſt, freely offered to us in the goſpel.

Q. 32. *What benefits do they that are effectually called partake of in this life?*

A. They that are effectually called do in this life partake of juſtification, adoption, and ſanctification, and the ſeveral benefits which in this life do either accompany or flow from them.

Q. 33. *What is juſtification?*

A. Juſtification is an act of God's free grace, wherein he pardoneth all our ſins, and accepteth us as righteous in his ſight, only for the righteouſneſs of Chriſt imputed to us, and received by faith alone.

Q. 34. *What is adoption?*

A. Adoption is an act of God's free grace whereby we are received into the number, and have a right to all the privileges of the fons of God.

Q. 35. *What is fanctification?*

A. Sanctification is the work of God's free grace, whereby we are renewed in the whole man, after the image of God, and are enabled more and more to die unto fin, and live unto righteoufnefs.

Q. 36. *What are the benefits which in this life do accompany or flow from juftification, adoption and fanctification?*

A. The benefits which in this life do accompany or flow from juftification, adoption and fanctification, are affurance of God's love, peace of confcience, joy in the holy Ghoft, increase of grace, and perfeverance therein to the end.

Q. 37. *What benefits do believers receive from Chrift at their death?*

A. The fouls of believers are at their death made perfect in holinefs, and do immediately pafs into glory, and their bodies being ftill united to Chrift do reft in their graves 'till the refurrection.

Q. 38. *What benefits do believers receive from Chriſt at the resurrection?*

A. At the reſurrection believers being raiſed up to glory, shall be openly acknowledged and acquitted in the day of judgment, and made perfectly bleſſed in the full enjoyment of God to all eternity.

Q. 39. *What is the duty which God requires of man?*

A. The duty which God requires of man, is obedience to his revealed will.

Q. 40. *What did God at firſt reveal to man for the rule of his obedience?*

A. The rule which God at firſt revealed to man for his obedience was the moral law.

Q. 41. *Where is the moral law ſummarily comprehended?*

A. The moral law is ſummarily comprehended in the ten commandments.

Q. 42. *What is the ſum of the ten commandments?*

A. The ſum of the ten commandments is, to love the Lord our God with all our heart, with all our ſoul, with all our ſtrength, and with all our mind, and our neighbour as ourſelves.

Q. 43. *What is the preface to the ten*

commandments ?

A. The preface to the ten command-ments is in thefe words, *I am the Lord thy God which have brought thee out of the land of* Egypt, *and out of the houfe of bondage.*

Q. 44. *What doth the preface to the ten commandments teach us ?*

A. The preface to the ten commandments teacheth us, that becaufe God is the Lord, and our God and Redeemer, therefore we are bound to keep all his commandments.

Q. 45. *Which is the first commandment ?*

A. The firft commandment is, *Thou fhalt have no other Gods before me.*

Q. 46. *What is required in the firft com-mandment ?*

A. The firft commandment requireth us to know and acknowledge God, to be the only true God, and our God, and to wor-fhip and glorify him accordingly.

Q. 47. *What is forbidden in the first com-mandment ?*

A. The firft commandment forbiddeth the denying or not worfhipping and glorify-ing the true God, as God, and our God, and the giving that worfhip and glory to any other which is due to him alone.

Q. 48. *What are we especially taught by those words* (before me) *in the first commandment?*

A. These words (*before me*) in the first commandment, teach us, that God who seeth all things, taketh notice of and is much displeased with the sin of having any other God.

Q. 49. *Which is the second commandment?*

A. The second commandment is, *Thou shalt not make unto thee any graven image, or the likeness of any thing that is in heaven above, or that is in the earth beneath, or that is in the water under the earth ; thou shalt not bow down thyself to them nor serve them, for I the Lord thy God am a jealous God, visiting the iniquities of the fathers upon the children, unto the third and fourth generation of them that hate me and shewing mercy unto thousands of them that love me & keep my commandments.*

Q. 50. *What is required in the second commandment?*

A. The second commandment requireth the receiving, observing, & keeping pure and entire all such religious worship and ordinances, as God hath appointed in his word.

Q. 51. *What is forbidden in the second commandment?*

A. The fecond commandment forbiddeth the worfhipping of God by images or any other way not appointed in his word.

Q. 52. *What are the reafons annexed to the fecond commandment ?*

A. The reafons annexed to the fecond commandment, are God's fovereignty over us, his propriety in us, and the zeal he hath to his own worfhip.

Q. 53. *Which is the third commandment ?*

A. The third commandment is, *Thou fhalt not take the name of the Lord thy God in vain, for the Lord will not hold him guilt- lefs, that taketh his name in vain.*

Q. 54. *What is required in the third commandment ?*

A. The third commandment requireth the holy and reverent ufe of God's names, titles, attributes, ordinances, word and works.

Q. 55. *What is forbidden in the third commandment ?*

A. The third commandment forbiddeth all profaning or abufing of any thing whereby God maketh himfelf known.

Q. 56. *What is the reafon annexed to the third commandment ?*

A. The reaſon annexed to the third commandment is, That however the breakers of
this commandment may eſcape puniſhment
from men, yet the Lord our God will not
ſuffer them to eſcape his righteous judgment.

Q. 57. *Which is the fourth commandment?*

A. The fourth commandment is, *Remember
the ſabbath day to keep it holy, ſix days ſhalt
thou labor and do all thy work, but the ſeventh day is the ſabbath of the Lord thy God,
in it thou ſhalt not do any work, thou nor thy
ſon, nor thy daughter, thy man-ſervant, nor
thy maid ſervant, nor thy cattle, nor the
ſtranger that is within thy gates, for in ſix
days the Lord made heaven and earth, the
ſea and all that in them is, and reſted the
ſeventh day, wherefore the Lord bleſſed the
ſabbath day and hallowed it.*

Q. 58. *What is required in the fourth
commandment?*

A. The fourth commandment requireth,
the keeping holy to God ſuch ſet times as
he hath appointed in his word, expreſſly one
whole day in ſeven to be an holy Sabbath
to himſelf.

Q. 59. *Which day of the ſeven hath God
appointed to be the weekly ſabbath?*

A. From the beginning of the world, to the refurrection of Chrift, God appointed the feventh day of the week to be the weekly fabbath, and the firft day of the week ever fince to continue to the end of the world, which is the Chriftian Sabbath.

Q. 60. *How is the fabbath to be fanctified ?*

A. The fabbath is to be fanctified by an holy refting all that day, even from fuch worldly employments and recreations as are lawful on other days, and fpending the whole time in public and private exercifes of God's worfhip, except fo much as is to be taken up in the works of neceffity and mercy.

Q. 61. *What is forbidden in the fourth commandment ?*

A. The fourth commandment forbiddeth, the omiffion or carelefs performance of the duties required, and the profaning the day by idlenefs, or doing that which is in itfelf finful, or by unneceffary thoughts, words or works, about worldly employments or recreations.

Q. 62. *What are the reafons annexed to the fourth commandment ?*

A. The reafons annexed to the fourth commandment, are God's allowing us fix days of the week for our own employment, his challenging a special propriety in the feventh, his own example, & his blefling the fabbath day.

Q. 63. *Which is the fifth commandment?*

A. The fifth commandment is, *Honor thy father and thy mother, that thy days may be long upon the land which the Lord thy God giveth thee.*

Q. 64. *What is required in the fifth commandment?*

A. The fifth commandment requireth the preferving the honor, and performing the duties belonging to every one in their feveral places and relations, as fuperiors, inferiors, or equals.

Q. 65. *What is forbidden in the fifth commandment?*

A. The fifth commandment forbiddeth the neglecting of, or doing any thing against the honour and duty which belongeth to every one in their feveral places and relations.

Q. 66. *What is the reason annexed to the fifth commandment?*

A. The reason annexed to the fifth commandment is a promife of long life and prof-perity, (as far as it fhall ferve for God's glory and their own good) to all fuch as keep this commandment.

Q. 67. *Which is the fixth commandment?*

A. The fixth commandment is, *Thou fhalt not kill.*

Q. 68. *What is required in the fixth commandment?*

A. The fixth commandment requireth all lawful endeavors to preferve our own life, and the life of others.

Q. 69. *What is forbidden in the fixth commandment?*

A. The fixth commandment forbiddeth the taking away of our own life, or the life of our neighbour unjuftly, and whatfoever tendeth thereunto.

Q. 70. *Which is the feventh commandment?*

A. The feventh commandment is, *Thou fhalt not commit adultery.*

Q. 71. *What is required in the feventh commandment?*

A. The feventh commandment requireth the prefervation of our own and our neighbor's chastity, in heart, speech & behaviour.

Q. 72. *What is forbidden in the feventh commandment?*

A. The feventh commandment forbiddeth all unchafte thoughts, words and actions.

Q. 73. *Which is the eighth commandment?*

A. The eighth commandment is, *Thou*

3*

ſhalt not ſteal.

Q. 74. *What is required in the eighth commandment?*

A. The eighth commandment requireth the lawful procuring & furthering the wealth and outward eſtate of ourſelves and others.

Q. 75. *What is forbidden in the eighth commandment?*

A. The eighth commandment forbiddeth whatſoever doth, or may unjuſtly hinder our own or our neighbour's wealth or outward eſtate.

Q. 76. *Which is the ninth commandment?*

A. The ninth commandment is, *Thou ſhalt not bear false witneſs againſt thy neighbour.*

Q. 77. *What is required in the ninth commandment?*

A. The ninth commandment requireth the maintaining and promoting of truth between man & man, & of our own & our neighbor's good name, eſpecially in witneſs bearing.

Q. 78. *What is forbidden in the ninth commandment?*

A. The ninth commandment. forbiddeth whatſoever is prejudicial to truth, or injurious to our own or our neighbor's good name.

Q. 79. *Which is the tenth commandment?*

A. The tenth commandment is, *Thou shalt not covet thy neighbour's house, thou shalt not covet thy neighbour's wife, nor his man-servant, nor his maid-servant, nor his ox, nor his afs, nor any thing that is thy neighbour's.*

Q. 80. *What is required in the tenth commandment?*

A. The tenth commandment requireth full contentment with our own condition, with a right and charitable frame of fpirit towards our neighbour, and all that is his.

Q. 81. *What is forbidden in the tenth commandment?*

A. The tenth commandment forbiddeth all difcontentment with our own eftate, envying or grieving at the good of our neighbour, and all inordinate motions and affections to any thing that is his.

Q. 82. *Is any man able perfectly to keep the commandments of God?*

A. No mere man fince the fall is able in this life perfectly to keep the commandments of God, but daily doth break them in thought, word and deed.

Q. 83. *Are all tranfgreffions of the law equally heinous?*

A. Some fins in themfelves, and by rea-

fon of feveral aggravations, are more heinous in the fight of God than others.

Q. 84. *What doth every fin deferve?*

A. Every fin deferves God's wrath & curfe
both in this life, and that which is to come.

Q. 85. *What doth God require of us that we
may efcape his wrath and curfe due to us for fin?*

A. To efcape the wrath and curfe of God
due to us for fin, God requireth of us faith in
Jefus Chrift, repentance unto life, with the di-
ligent ufe of all outward means whereby Chrift
communicateth to us the benefits of redemption. Q. 86. *What is faith in Jefus Chrift?*

A. Faith in Jefus Chrift is a faving grace
whereby we receive & reft upon him alone for
falvation as he is offered to us in the gofpel.

Q. 87. *What is repentance unto life?*

A. Repentance unto life is a faving grace,
whereby a finner out of the true fenfe of his
fin and apprehenfion of the mercy of God in
Chrift, doth with grief and hatred of his fin
turn from it unto God, with full purpofe of
and endeavours after new obedience.

Q. 88. *What are the outward and ordinary means whereby Chrift communicateth to
us the benefits of redemption?*

A. The outward and ordinary means where

by Chrift communicateth to us the benefits of redemption, are his ordinances, efpecially the word, facraments and prayer ; all which are made effectual to the elect for falvation.

Q. 89. *How is the word made effectual to falvation ?*

A. The fpirit of God maketh the reading, but efpecially the preaching of the word an effectual means of convincing and converting finners, and of building them up in holinefs and comfort, through faith unto falvation.

Q. 90. *How is the word to be read and heard that it may become effectual to falvation?*

A. That the word may become effectual to falvation, we must attend thereunto with diligence, preparation and prayer, receive it with faith and love, lay it up in our hearts, and practice it in our lives.

Q. 91 *How do the facraments become effectual means of falvation ?*

A. The facraments become effectual means of falvation not from any virtue in them or in him that doth adminifter them, but only by the blefling of Chrift, and the working of the Spirit in them that by faith receive them.

Q. 92. *What is a facrament ?*

A. A facrament is an holy ordinance inſtituted by Chriſt, wherein by ſenſible ſigns, Chriſt & the benefits of the new covenant are repreſented ſealed and applied to believers.

Q. 93. *What are the ſacraments of the New Teſtament?*

A. The ſacraments of the New Teſtament are baptiſm and the Lord's ſupper.

Q. 94. *What is baptism?*

A. Baptiſm is a ſacrament wherein the waſhing of water in the name of the Father and of the Son and of the Holy Ghoſt, doth ſignify and ſeal our ingrafting into Chriſt and partaking of the benefits of the covenant of grace, & our engagements to be the Lord's.

Q. 95. *To whom is baptism to be administered?*

A. Baptiſm is not to be adminiſtered to any that are out of the viſible church, till they profeſs their faith in Chriſt, and obedience to him, but the infants of ſuch as are members of the viſible church are to be baptized.

Q. 96. *What is the Lord's ſupper?*

A. The Lord's ſupper is a ſacrament, wherein by giving and receiving bread and wine according to Chriſt's appointment, his death is ſhewed forth, and the worthy receivers are not after a corporal and carnal manner, but by faith made partakers of his body and blood, with all his benefits, to their fpiritual nourifhment and growth in grace.

Q. 97. *What is required in the worthy receiving the Lord's fupper?*

A. It is required of them that would worthily partake of the Lord's fupper, that they examine themfelves of their knowledge to difcern the Lord's body, of their faith to feed upon him, of their repentance, love and new obedience, left coming unworthily, they eat and drink judgment to themfelves.

Q. 98. *What is prayer?*

A. Prayer is an offering up of our defires to God for things agreeable to his will, in the name of Chrift, with confeffion of our fins, & thankful acknowledgment of his mercies.

Q. 99. *What rule hath God given for our direction in prayer?*

A. The whole word of God is of ufe to direct us in prayer but the fpecial rule of direction is that form of prayer which Chrift taught his difciples commonly called, *The Lord's Prayer.*

Q. 100. *What doth the preface of the Lord's prayer teach us?*

A. The preface of the Lord's prayer which is *Our Father which art in heaven,* teacheth us, to draw near to God with all holy reverence and confidence, as children to a father, able and ready to help us, and that we fhould pray with and for others.

Q.101. *What do we pray for in the first petition?*

A. In the firft petition, which is, *Hallowed be thy name*, we pray that God would enable us and others to glorify him in all that whereby he makes himfelf known, and that he would difpofe all things to his own glory.

Q. 102. *What do we pray for in the fecond petition?*

A. In the fecond petition, which is, *Thy kingdom come*, we pray that fatan's kingdom may be deftroyed, the kingdom of grace may be advanced, ourfelves and others bro't into it, and kept in it, and that the kingdom of glory may be haftened.

Q. 103. *What do we pray for in the third petition?*

A. In the third petition, which is, *Thy will be done on earth as it is in heaven*, we pray that God by his grace would make us able and willing to know, obey and fubmit to his will in all things, as the angels do in heaven.

Q. 104. *What do we pray for in the fourth petition?*

A. In the fourth petition, which is, *Give*

us this day our daily bread, we pray, that of God's free gift we may receive a competent portion of the good things of this life, and enjoy his blefling with them.

Q. 105. *What do we pray for in the fifth petition ?*

A. In the fifth petition, which is, *And forgive us our debts as we forgive our debtors*, we pray that God for Chrift's fake, would freely pardon all our fins, which we are the rather encouraged to afk, becaufe by his grace we are enabled from the heart to forgive others.

Q. 106. *What do we pray for in the fixth petition ?*

A. In the fixth petition, which is, *And lead us not into temptation, but deliver us from evil*, we pray that God would cither keep us from being tempted to fin, or fupport and deliver us when we are tempted.

Q. 107. *What doth the conclufion of the Lord's prayer teach us ?*

A. The conclufion of the Lord's prayer, which is, *For thine is the kingdom, and the power, and the glory, forever*, A M E N, teacheth us, to take our encouragement in prayer from God only, and in our prayers to praife him, afcribing kingdom, power and glory

to him, and in teſtimony of our deſire and
aſſurance to be heard, we ſay, A M E N.

*Bleſſed are they that do his commandments
that they may have right to the tree of
life, and may enter in through the gates
into the city.* Rev. xxii. 14.

✹✹✹✹✹✹✹✹✹✹✹✹✹✹✹✹✹✹✹✹✹✹

S P I R I T U A L   M I L K

F O R

American B A B E S,

Drawn out of the Breaſts of both *Teſtaments*

for their Souls Nouriſhment.

By J O H N   C O T T O N.

Q *W HAT hath God done for you?*
   A. God hath made me, he keep-
eth me, and he can ſave me.

Q. *What is God?*

A. God is a Spirit of himſelf & for himſelf.

Q. *How many Gods be there?*

A. There is but one God in three Perſons,
the Father, and the Son, and the Holy Ghoſt

Q. *How did God make you?*

A. In my firſt parents holy and righteous.

Q. *Are you then born holy and righteous*.

A. No, my firſt father ſinned and I in him.

Q. *Are you then born a ſinner?*

A. I was conceived in ſin, & born in iniquity

Q. *What is your birth ſin?*

A. Adam's ſin imputed to me, and a corrupt nature dwelling in me.

Q. *What is your corrupt nature?*

A. My corrupt nature is empty of grace, bent unto ſin, only unto ſin, and that continually.

Q. *What is ſin?*

A. Sin is a tranſgreſſion of the law.

Q. *How many commandments of the law be there?*   A. Ten.

Q. *What is the first commandment?*

A. Thou ſhalt have no other Gods before me.

Q. *What is the meaning of this commandment?*

A. That we ſhould worſhip the only **true** God, and no other beſides him.

Q. *What is the ſecond commandment?*

A. Thou ſhalt not make to thyſelf any graven image, &c.

Q. *What is the meaning of this commandment?*

A. That we ſhould worſhip the only **true** God, with true worſhip, ſuch as he hath or dained, not ſuch as man hath invented.

Q. *What is the third commandment?*

A. Thou ſhalt not take the name of the Lord thy God in vain.

Q. What is meant by the name of God?

A. God himſelf & the good things of God, whereby he is known as a man by his name, and his attributes, worſhip, word and works.

Q. What is it not to take his name in vain?

A. To make uſe of God & the good things of God to his glory, and our own good, not vainly, not irreverently, not unprofitably.

Q. Which is the fourth commandment?

A. Remember that thou keep holy the ſabbath day.

Q. What is the meaning of this commandment?

A. That we ſhould reſt from labor, and much more from play on the Lord's day, that we may draw nigh to God in holy duties.

Q. What is the fifth commandment?

A Honor thy father and thy mother, that thy days may be long in the land which the Lord thy God giveth thee.

Q. What are meant by father and mother?

A. All our ſuperiors whether in family, ſchool, church and common wealth.

Q. What is the honor due unto them?

A. Reverence, obedience, and (when I am able) recompence.

Q. *What is the fixth commandment?*

A. Thou fhalt do no murder.

Q. *What is the meaning of this commandment?*

A. That we fhould not fhorten the life or health of ourfelves or others, but preferve both

Q. *What is the feventh commandment?*

A. Thou fhalt not commit adultery.

Q. *What is the fin here forbidden?*

A. To defile ourfelves or others with unclean lufts.

Q. *What is the duty here commanded?*

A. Chaftity to poffefs our veffels in holinefs and honor.

Q. *What is the eighth commandment?*

A. Thou fhalt not fteal.

Q. *What is the ftealth here forbidden?*

A. To take away another man's goods without his leave, or to fpend our own without benefit to ourfelves or others.

Q. *What is the duty here commanded?*

A. To get our goods honeftly, to keep them fafely, and fpend them thriftily.

Q. *What is the ninth commandment?*

A. Thou fhalt not bear falfe witnefs againft thy neighbour.

Q. *What is the fin here forbidden?*

A. To lie falfely, to think or fpeak **untru**ly of ourfelves or others.

Q. What is the duty here required?

A. Truth and faithfulnefs.

Q. What is the tenth commandment?

A. Thou fhalt not covet, &c.

Q. What is the coveting here forbidden?

A. Luft after the things of other men, and want of contentment with our own.

Q. Whether have you kept all thefe commandments?

A. No, I and all men are finners.

Q. What are the wages of fin?

A. Death and damnation.

Q. How then look you to be faved?

A. Only by Jefus Chrift.

Q. Who is Jefus Chrift?

A. The eternal Son of God, who for our fakes became man, that he might redeem & fave us.

Q. How doth Chrift redeem and fave us?

A. By his righteous life, and bitter death, and glorious refurrection to life again.

Q. How do we come to have a part & fellowfhip with Chrift in his death & refurrection?

A. By the power of his word and fpirit, which brings us to him, and keeps us in him.

Q. What is the word?

A. The holy fcriptures of the prophets and apoftles, the old and new teftament, the law and gofpel.

Q. How doth the miniftry of the law bring you toward Chrift?

A. By bringing me to know my fin, and the wrath of God, againft me for it.

Q. What are you hereby the nearer to Chrift?

A. So I come to feel my curfed eftate and need of a Saviour.

Q. How doth the miniftry of the Gofpel help you in this curfed eftate?

A. By humbling me yet more, and then raifing me out of this eftate.

Q. How doth the miniftry of the Gofpel humble you yet more?

A. By revealing the grace of the Lord Jefus in dying to fave finners, and yet convincing me of my fin in not believing on him, and of my utter infufficiency to come to him, and fo I feel myfelf utterly loft.

Q. How doth the miniftry of the gospel raife you up out of this loft eftate to come to Chrift?

A. By teaching me the value and virtue of the death of Chrift, and the riches of his grace to loft finners by revealing the promife of grace to fuch, and by miniftring the Spirit of grace to apply Chrift, and his promife of grace unto myfelf, and to keep me in him.

Q. *How doth the Spirit of grace apply Chrift & his promife grace unto you and keep you in him?*

A. By begetting in me faith to receive him, prayer to call upon him, repentance to mourn after him, and new obedience to ferve him.

Q. *What is faith?*

A. Faith is the grace of the Spirit, whereby I deny myfelf, and believe on Chrift for righteoufnefs and falvation.

Q. *What is prayer?*

A. It is calling upon God in the name of Chrift by the help of the Holy Ghoft, accor ding to the will of God.

Q. *What is repentance?*

A. Repentance is a grace of the Spirit, whereby I loath my fins, and myfelf for them and confefs them before the Lord, and mourn after Chrift for the pardon of them, and for grace to ferve him in newnefs of life.

Q. *What is the newnefs of life, or new obedience?*

A. Newnefs of life is a grace of the Spirit, whereby I forfake my former luft & vain company, and walk before the Lord in the light of his word, and in the communion of faints.

Q. *What is the communion of faints?*

A. It is the fellowſhip of the church in the bleſſings of the covenant of grace, and the ſeals thereof.   Q. *What is the church?*

A. It is a congregation of ſaints joined together in the bond of the covenant, to wor-ſhip the Lord, and to edify one another in all his holy ordinances.

Q, *What is the bond of the covenant by which the church is joined together?*

A. It is the profeſſion of that covenant which God has made with his faithful people, to be a God unto them, and to their ſeed.

Q. *What doth the Lord bind his people to in this covenant?*

A. To give up themſelves & their ſeed firſt to the Lord to be his people, & then to the el-ders & brethren of the church to ſet forward the worſhip of God & their mutual edification.

Q. *How do they give up themſelves and their ſeed to the Lord?*

A. By receiving thro' faith the Lord & his covenant to themſelves, & to their ſeed & ac-cordingly walking themſelves & training up their children in the ways of the covenant.

Q. *How do they give up themſelves and their ſeed to the elders and brethren of the church?*

A. By confeſſing of their ſins, and profeſ-

4

fion of their faith, and of their fubjection to the gofpel of Chrift; and fo they and their feed are received into the fellowfhip of the church and the feals thereof.

Q. *What are the feals of the covenant now in the days of the gofpel?*

A. Baptifm and the Lord's Supper.

Q. *What is done for you in baptifm?*

A. In baptifm the wafhing with water is a fign and feal of my wafhing in the blood and fpirit of Chrift, and thereby of my ingrafting into Chrift, of the pardon and cleanfing of my fins, of my raifing up out of afflictions, and alfo of my refurrection from the dead at the laft day.

Q. *What is done for you in the Lord's fupper?*

A. In the Lord's fupper, the receiving of the bread broken and the wine poured out is a fign and feal of my receiving the communion of the body of Chrift broken for me, and of his blood fhed for me, and thereby of my growth in Chrift, and the pardon and healing of my fins, of the fellowfhip of the Spirit, of my ftrengthening and quickening in grace, and of my fitting together with Chrift on his throne of glory at the laft judgment.

Q. *What was the refurrection from the*

dead, which was *fealed up to you in baptism ?*

A. When Chrift fhall come in his laft judgment, all that are in their graves fhall rife again, both the juft and unjuft.

Q. What is the judgment, which is fealed up to you in the Lord's supper ?

A. At the laft day we fhall all appear before the judgment feat of Chrift, to give an account of our works, and receive our reward according to them.

Q. What is the reward that fhall then be given?

A. The righteous fhall go into life eternal, and the wicked fhall be caft into everlafting fire with the Devil and his angels.

A DIALOGUE *between* CHRIST, YOUTH, *and the* Devil.   YOUTH.

THofe days which God to me doth fend,
    In pleafure I'm refolv'd to fpend ;
Like as the birds in th' lovely spring,
Sit chirping on the bough, and fing ;
Who ftraining forth thofe warbling notes,
Do make fweet mufic in their throats,
So I refolve in this my prime,
In fports and plays to fpend my time.
Sorrow and grief I'll put away,
Such things agree not with my day:

From clouds my morning fhall be free,
And nought on earth fhall trouble me.
I will embrace each fweet delight,
This earth affords me day and night:
Though parents grieve and me correct,
Yet I their counsel will reject.

Devil.

The refolution which you take,
Sweet youth it doth me merry make.
If thou my counsel wilt embrace,
And fhun the ways of truth and grace,
And learn to lie, and curfe and swear.
And be as proud as any are;
And with thy brothers wilt fall out,
And fifters with vile language flout ·
Yea, fight and fcratch, and alfo bite,
Then in thee I will take delight.
If thou wilt but be rul'd by me,
An artift thou fhalt quickly be,
In all my ways which lovely are,
Ther'e few with thee who fhall compare.
Thy parents always difobey;
Don't mind at all what they do fay:
And alfo pout and fullen be,
And thou fhalt be a child for me.
When others read, be thou at play,
Think not on God, don't sigh nor pray

Nor be thou such a silly fool,
To mind thy book or go to school;
But play the truant; fear not I
Will straitway help you to a lie,
Which will excuse thee from the same,
From being whipp'd and from all blame;
Come bow to me, uphold my crown,
And I'll thee raise to high renown.

YOUTH.

These motions I will cleave unto,
And let all other counsels go;
My heart against my parents now,
Shall harden'd be, and will not bow:
I won't submit at all to them,
But all good counsels will condemn,
And what I list that do will I,
And stubborn be continually.

CHRIST.

Wilt thou, O youth make such a choice,
And thus obey the devil's voice!
Curst sinful ways wilt thou embrace,
And hate the ways of truth and grace?
Wilt thou to me a rebel prove?
And from thy parents quite remove
Thy heart also? Then shalt thou see,
What will e'er long become of thee.
Come, think on God, who did thee make,

4*

And at his prefence dread and quake,
Remember him now in thy youth,
And let thy foul take hold of truth :
The Devil and his ways defy,
Believe him not, he doth but lie :
His ways feem fweet, but youth beware,
He for thy foul hath laid a fnare.
His fweet will into bitter turn,
If in thofe ways thou ftill wilt run,
He will thee into pieces tear,
Like lions which moft hungry are.
Grant me thy heart, thy folly leave,
And from this lion I'll thee fave ;
And thou fhalt have fweet joy from me,
Which fhall laft to eternity.

YOUTH.

My heart fhall chear me in my youth,
I'll have my frolicks in good truth,
What e'er feems lovely in mine eye.
Myfelf I cannot it deny.
In my own ways I ftill will walk,
And take delight among young folk,
Who fpend their days in joy and mirth,
Nothing like that I'm fure on earth :
Thy ways, O Chrift! are not for me,
They with my age do not agree.
If I unto thy laws fhould cleave,

No more good days then fhould I have.
CHRIST.

Woul'ft thou live long and good days fee
Refrain from all iniquity :
True good alone doth from me flow,
It can't be had in things below.
Are not my ways, O youth! for thee,
Then thou fhalt never happy be ;
Nor ever fhall thy foul obtain,
True good, whilft thou doft here remain

YOUTH.

To thee, O Chrift, I'll not adhere,
What thou fpeak'ft of does not appear
Lovely to me I cannot find,
'Tis good to fet or place my mind
On ways whence many forrows fpring
And to the flefh fuch croffes bring,
Don't trouble me, I muft fulfil,
My flefhly mind, and have my wil'.

CHRIST.

Unto thyfelf then I'll thee leave,
That Satan may thee wholly have :
Thy heart in fin fhall harden'd be,
And blinded in iniquity.
And then in wrath I'll cut thee down
Like af the grafs and flowers mown.
And to thy woe thou fhalt efpy,

Childhood and youth are vanity;
For all fuch things I'll make thee know
To judgment thou fhall come alfo.
In hell at laft thy foul fhall burn,
When thou thy finful race haft run.
Confider this, think on thy end
Left God do thee in pieces rend.

YOUTH.

Amazed, Lord! I now begin,
O help me and I'll leave my fin:
I tremble, and do greatly fear,
To think upon what I do hear.
Lord! I religious now will be,
And I'll from Satan turn to thee.

Devil.

Nay, foolifh youth, don't change thy mind,
Unto fuch thoughts be not inclin'd.
Come, cheer up thy heart, roufe up, be glad.
There is no hell; why art thou fad?
Eat, drink, be merry with thy friend,
For when thou dieft, that's thy laft end.

YOUTH.

Such thoughts as thefe I can't receive,
Becaufe God's word I do believe;
None fhall in this deftroy my faith,
Nor do I mind what Satan faith.

Devil.

Although to thee herein I yield,
Yet e'er long I fhall win the field.
That there's a heaven I can't deny,
Yea, and a hell of mifery:
That heaven is a lovely place
I can't deny; 'tis a clear cafe;
And eafy 'tis for to come there,
Therefore take thou no further care,
All human laws do thou obferve,
And from old cuftoms never fwerve;
Do not oppofe what great men fay,
And thou fhalt never go aftray.
Thou may'ft be drunk, and fwear and curfe,
And finners like thee ne'er the worfe;
At any time thou may'ft repent;
'Twill ferve when all thy days are fpent.

CHRIST.

Take heed or elfe thou art undone;
Thefe thoughts are from the wicked One,
Narrow's the way that leads to life,
Who walk therein do meet with ftrife.
Few fhall be faved, young man know,
Moft do unto deftruction go.
If righteous ones fcarce faved be,
What will at laft become of thee!
Oh! don't reject my precious call,
Left suddenly in hell thou fall;

Unlefs you foon converted be,
God's kingdom thou fhalt never fee.
YOUTH.
Lord, I am now at a great ftand :
If I fhould yield to thy command,
My comrades will me much deride,
And never more will me abide.
Moreover, this I alfo know,
Thou can'ft at laft great mercy fhow.
When I am old, and pleafure gone,
Then what thou fay'ft I'll think upon.
CHRIST.
Nay, hold vain youth, thy time is fhort,
I have thy breath, I'll end thy fport;
Thou fhalt not live till thou art old,
Since thou in fin art grown fo bold.
I in thy youth grim death will fend,
And all thy fports fhall have an end.
YOUTH.
I am too young, alas to die,
Let death fome old grey head efpy.
O fpare me, and I will amend,
And with thy grace my foul befriend,
Or elfe I am undone alas,
For I am in a woful cafe.
CHRIST.
When I did call, you would not hear,

But didſt to me turn a deaf ear;
And now in thy calamity,
I will not mind nor hear thy cry;
Thy day is paſt, begone from me,
Thou who didſt love iniquity,
Above thy foul and Saviour dear;
Who on the croſs great pains did bear,
My mercy thou didſt much abuſe,
And all good counſel didſt refuſe,
Juſtice will therefore vengeance take,
And thee a ſad example make.

YOUTH.

O ſpare me, Lord, forbear thy hand,
Don't cut me off who trembling ſtand,
Begging for mercy at thy door,
O let me have but one year more.

CHRIST.

If thou ſome longer time ſhould have,
Thou wouldſt again to folly cleave:
Therefore to thee I will not give,
One day on earth longer to live.

Death.

Youth, I am come to fetch thy breath,
And carry thee to th' ſhades of death,
No pity on thee can I ſhow,
Thou haſt thy God offended ſo.
Thy ſoul and body I'll divide,

Thy body in the grave I'll hide,
And thy dear foul in hell muft lie
With Devils to eternity.

The conclufion.

Thus end the days of woful youth,
Who won't obey nor mind the truth;
Nor hearken to what preachers fay,
But do their parents difobey.
They in their youth go down to hell,
Under eternal wrath to dwell.
Many don't live out half their days,
For cleaving unto finful ways.

The late Reverend and Venerable Mr. NA-
THANIEL CLAP, *of* Newport *on* Rhode
Ifland; *his Advice to children.*

GOOD children fhould remember daily,
God their Creator, Redeemer, and
Sanctifier; to believe in, love and ferve him;
their parents to obey them in the LORD;
their bible and catechifm; their baptifm;
the LORD's day; the LORD's death and refurrection; their own death and refurrection; and the day of judgment, when all that
are not fit for heaven muft be fent to hell.
And they fhould pray to GOD in the name
of CHRIST, for faving grace

CPSIA information can be obtained
at www.ICGtesting.com
Printed in the USA
LVHW100757030621
689199LV00001B/19